ALIENS COLORING BOOK

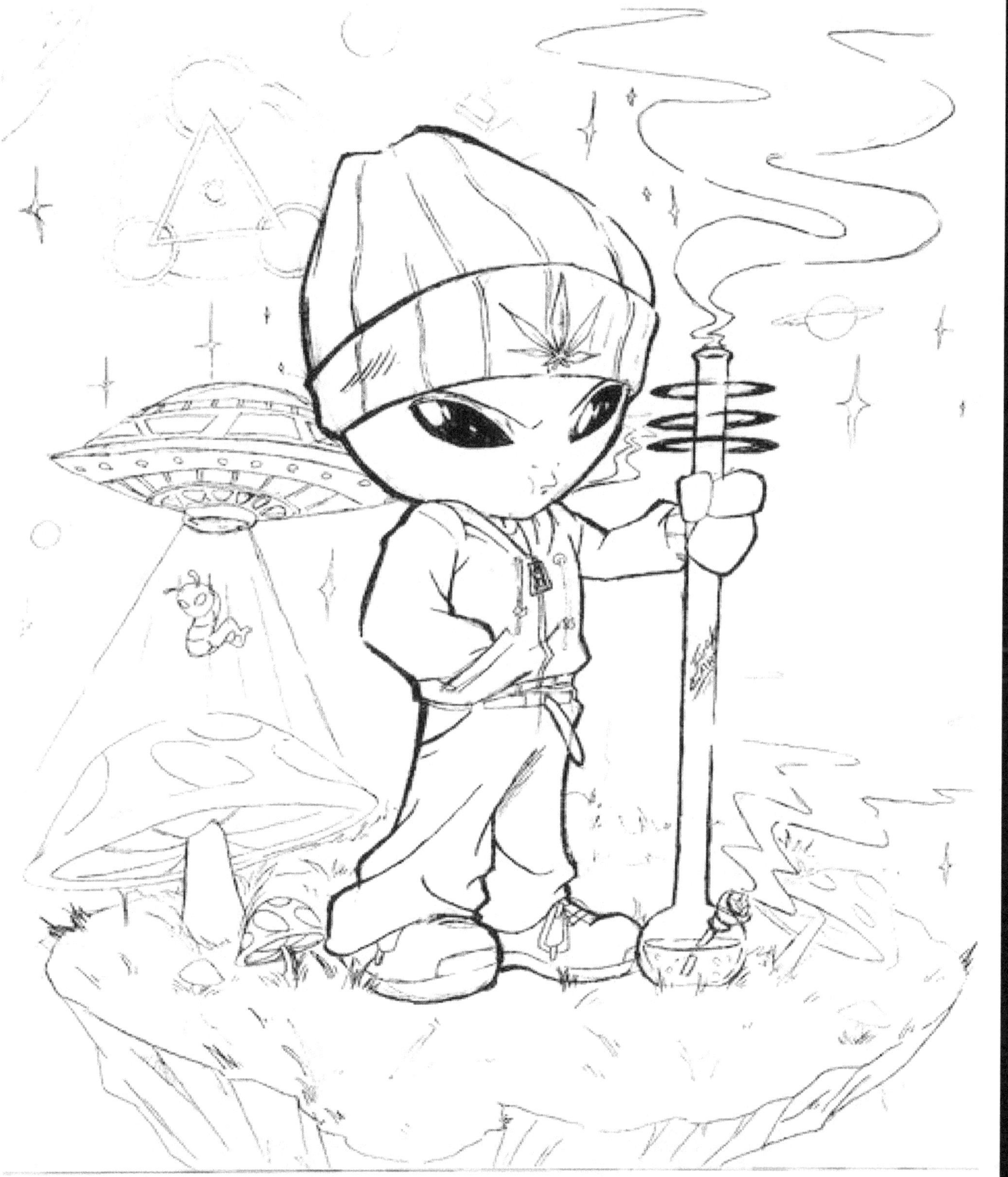

TEST YOUR COLOR

TEST YOUR COLOR

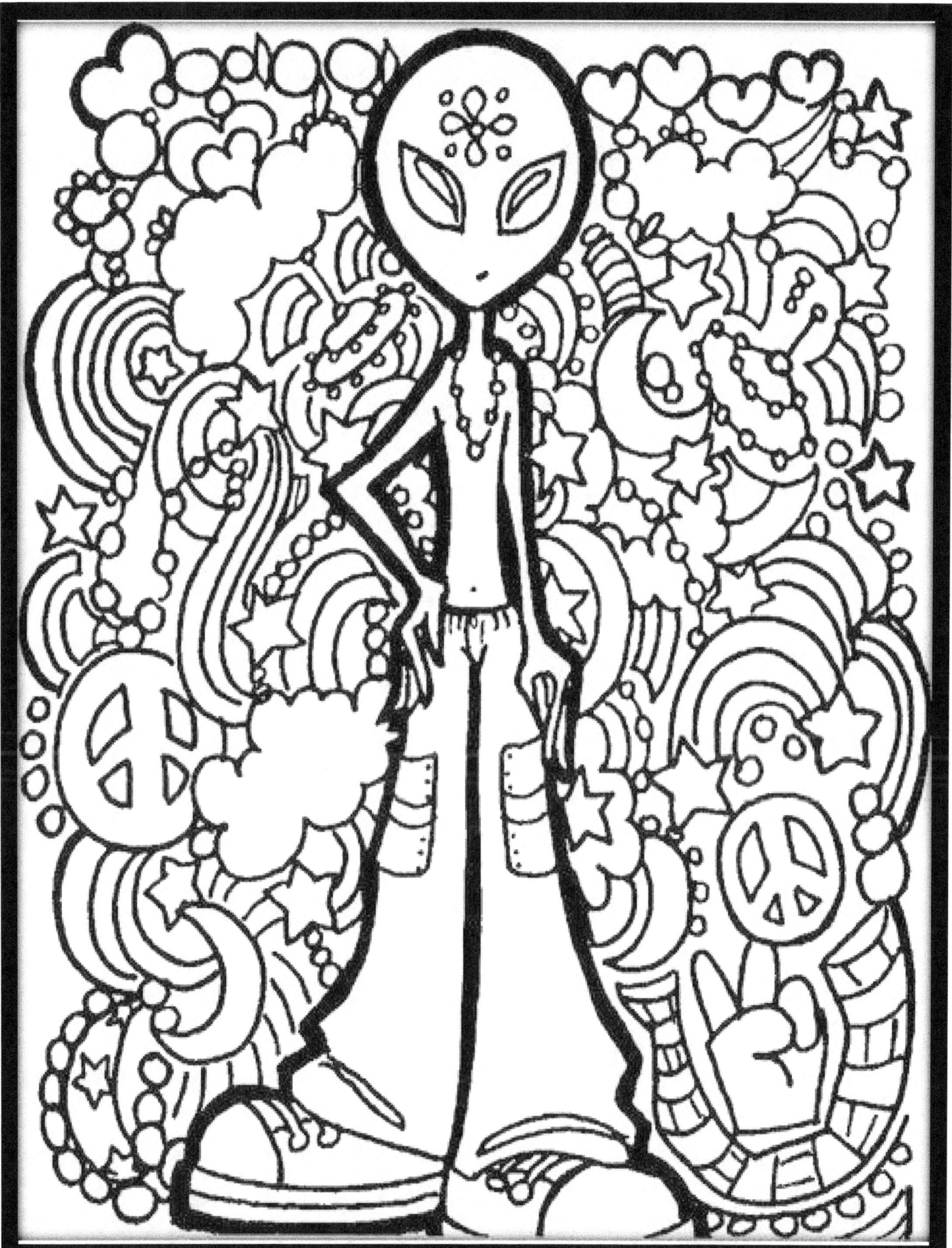

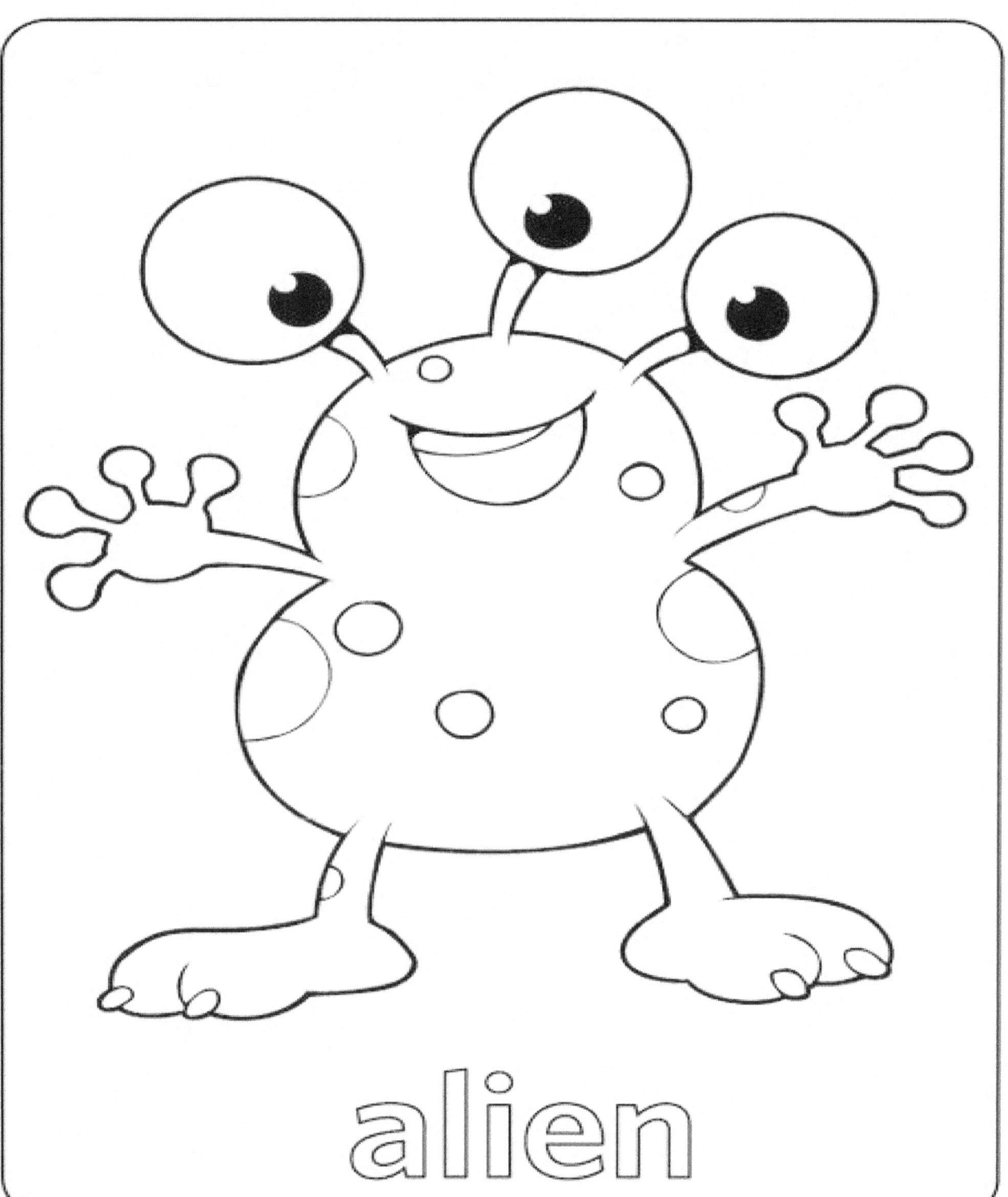

alien

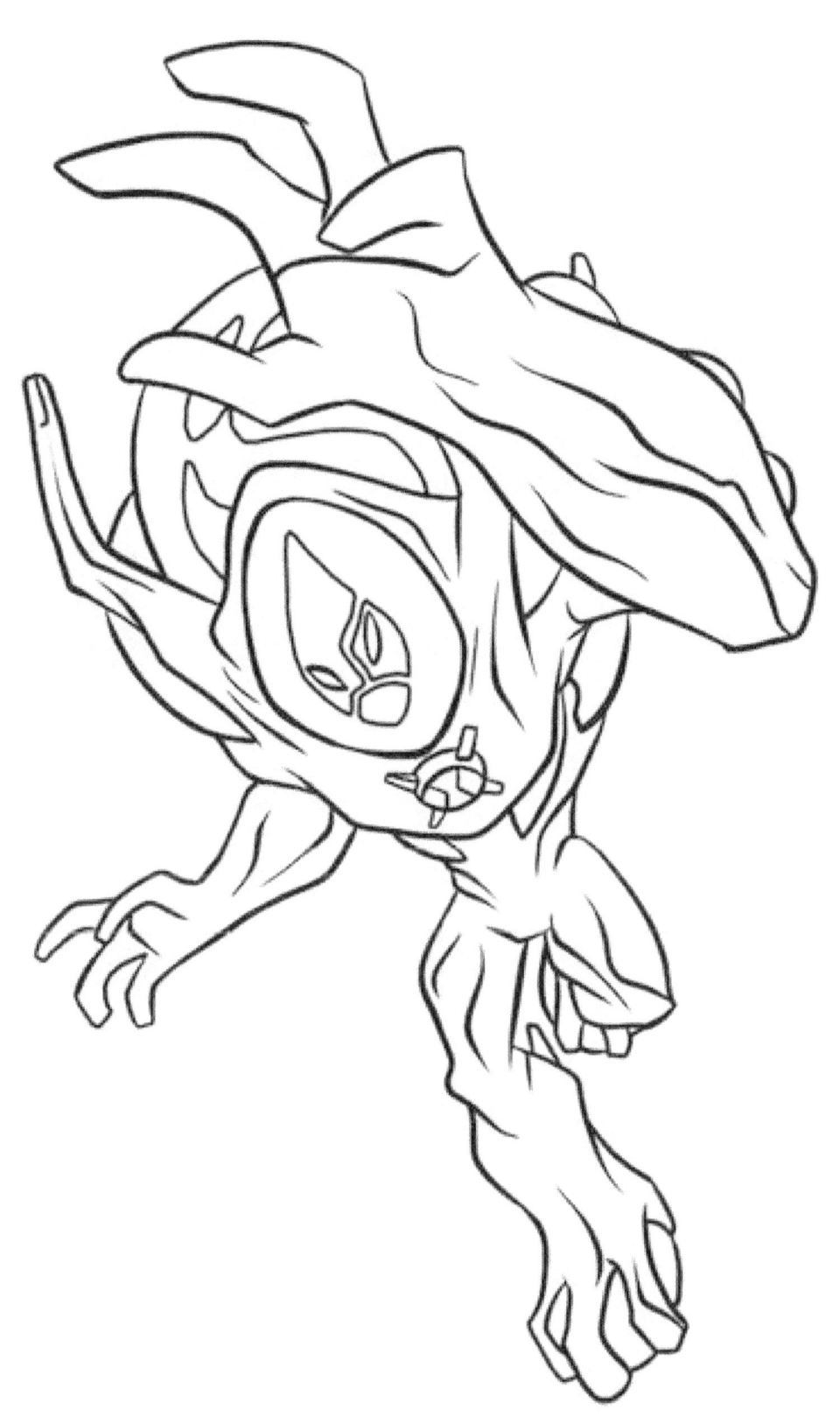

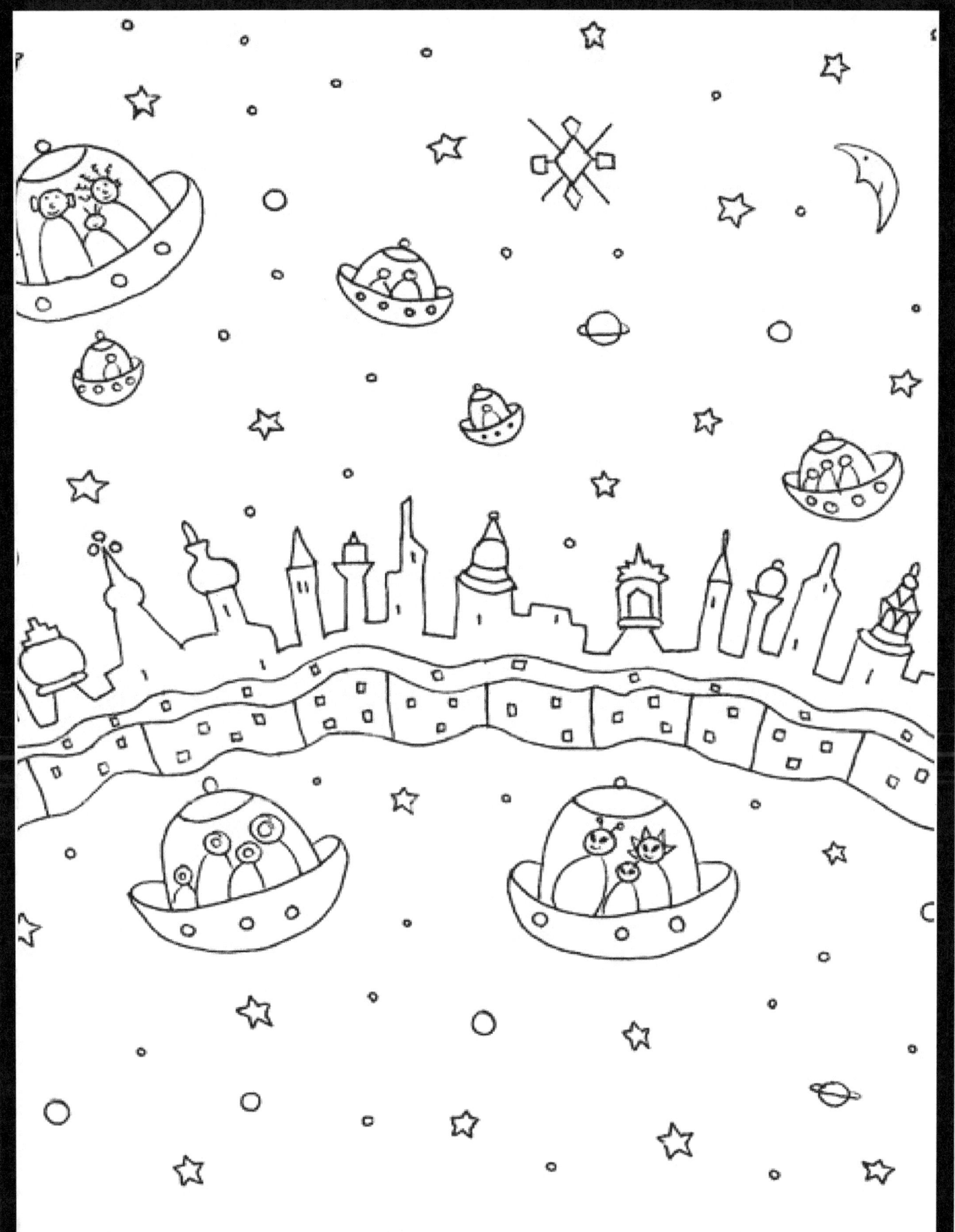

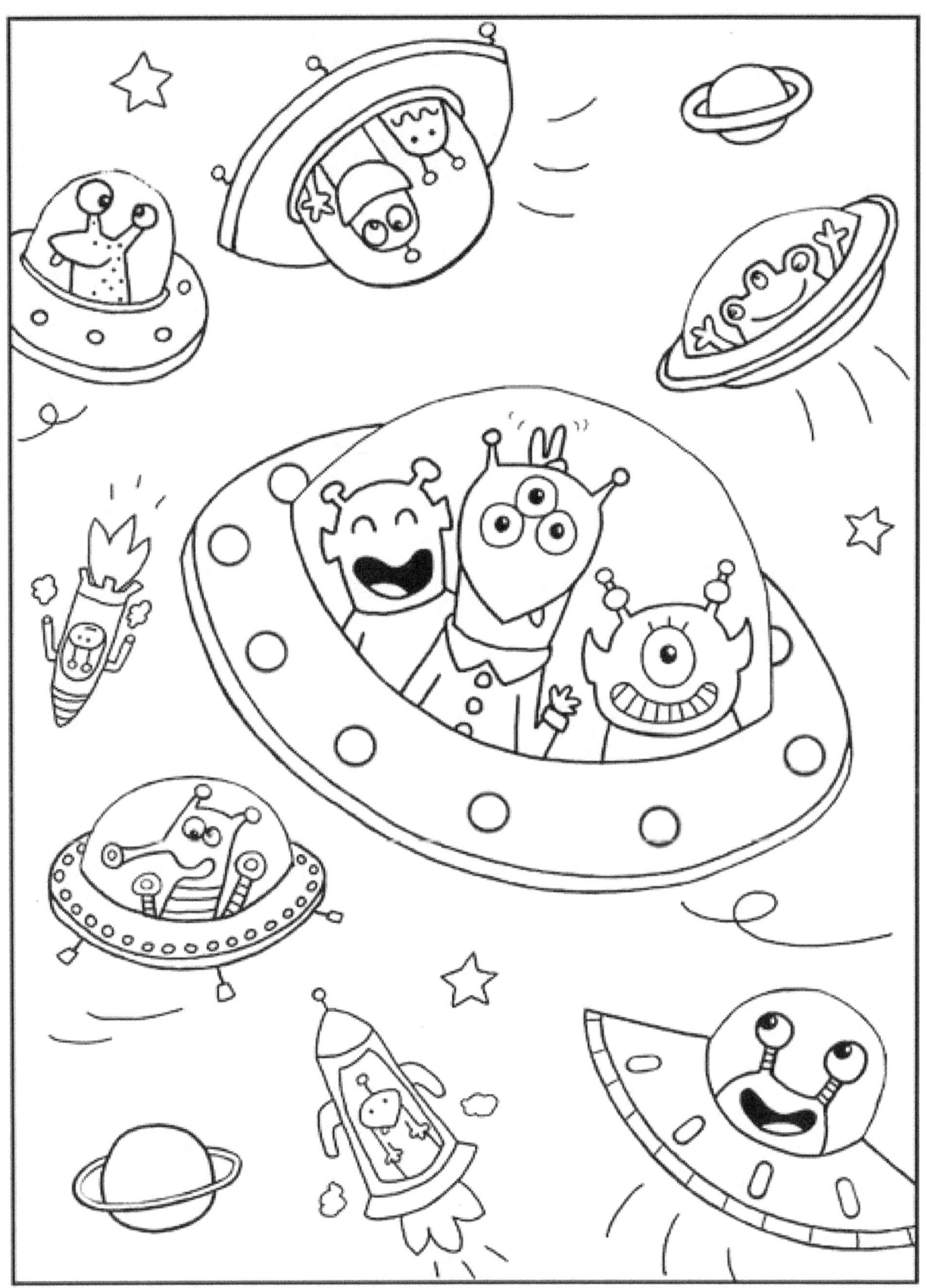

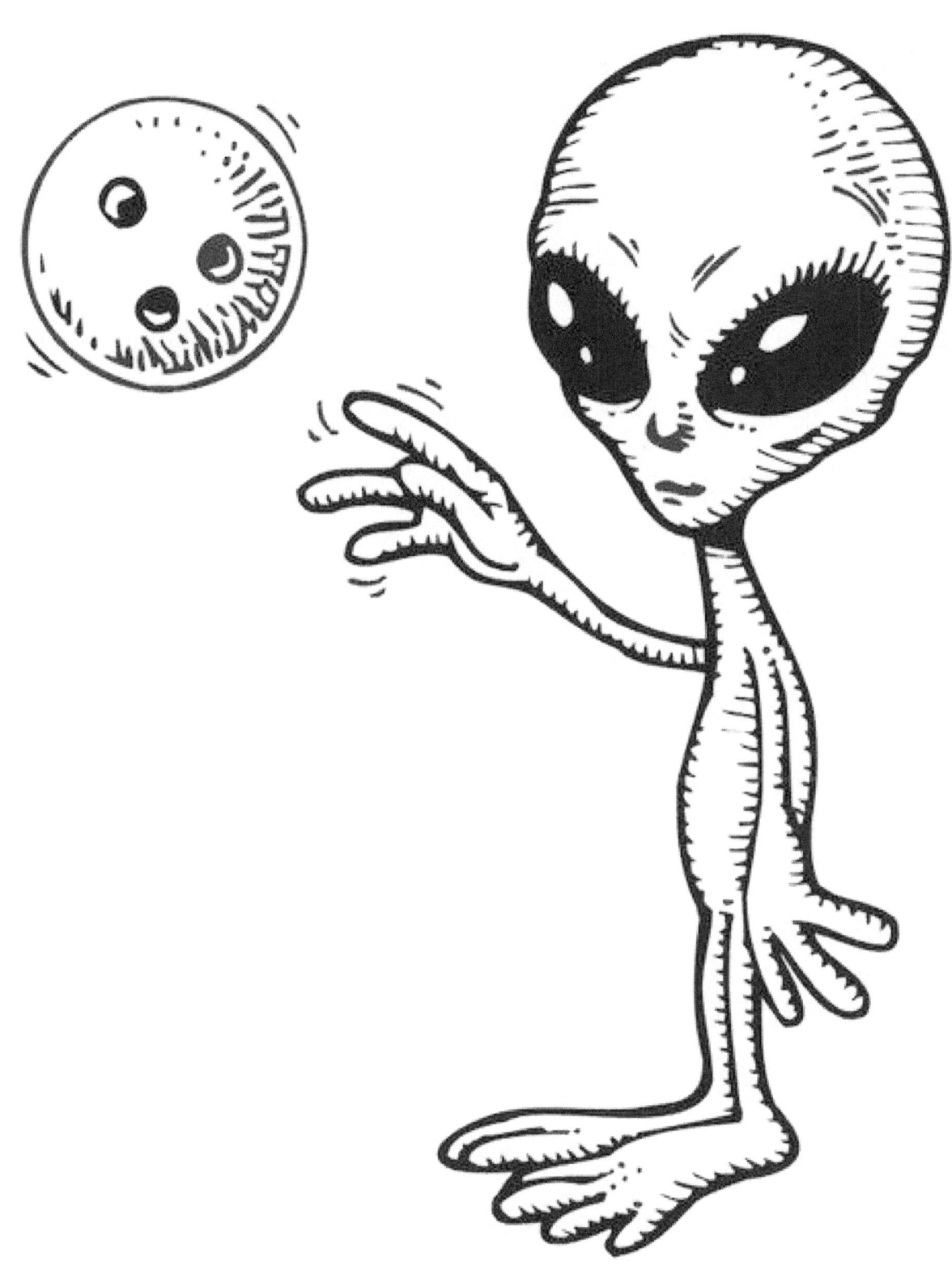

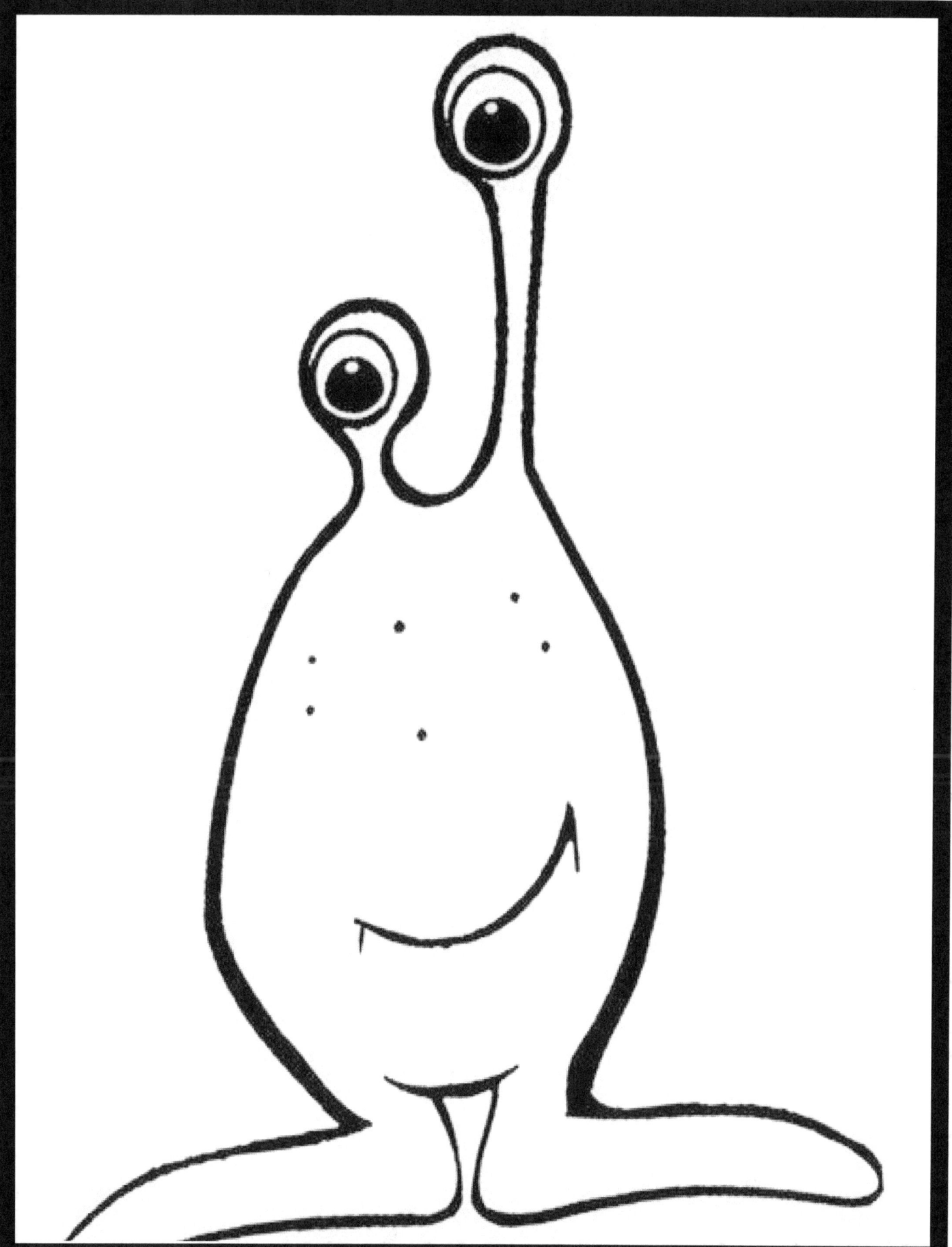

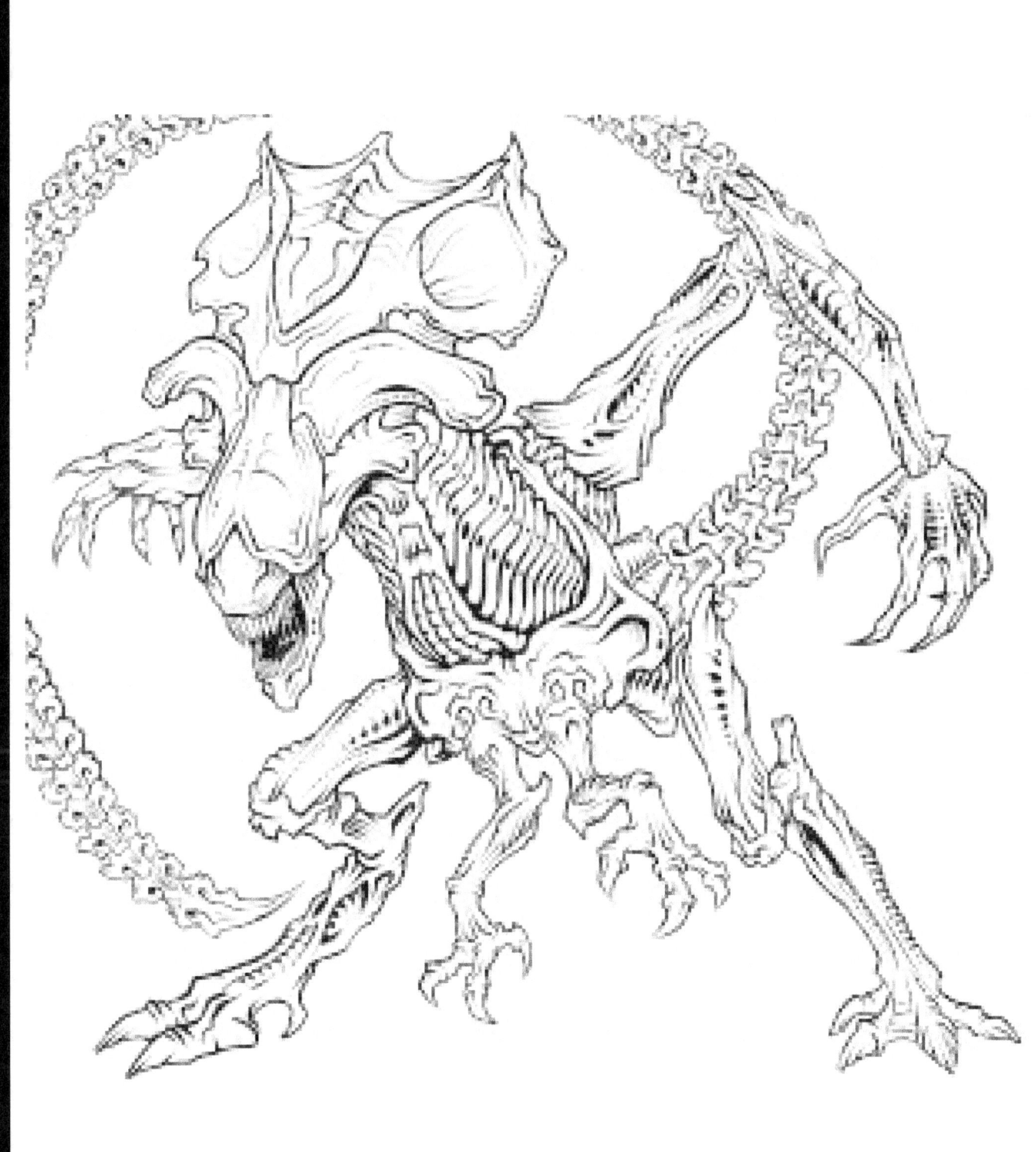

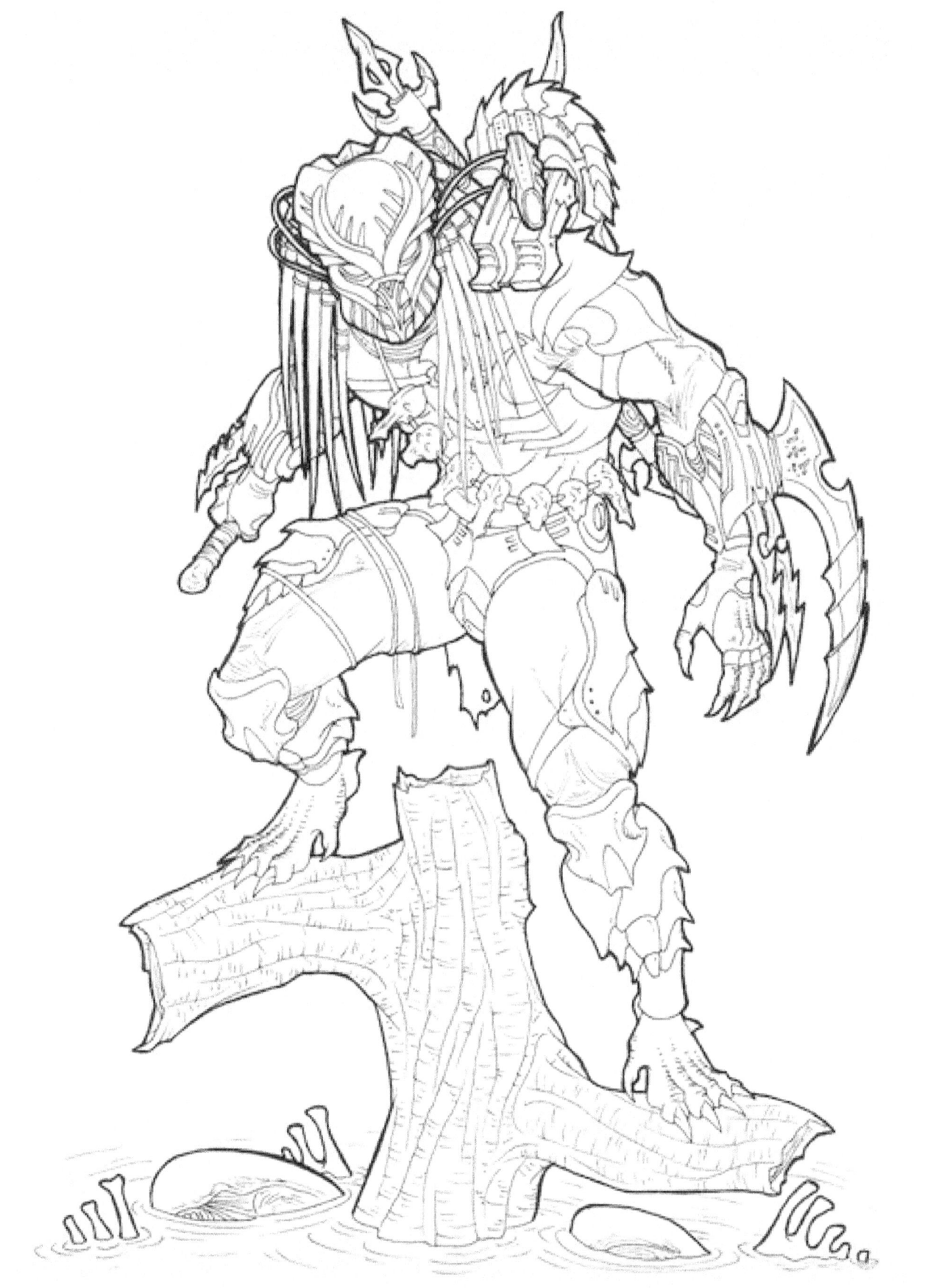

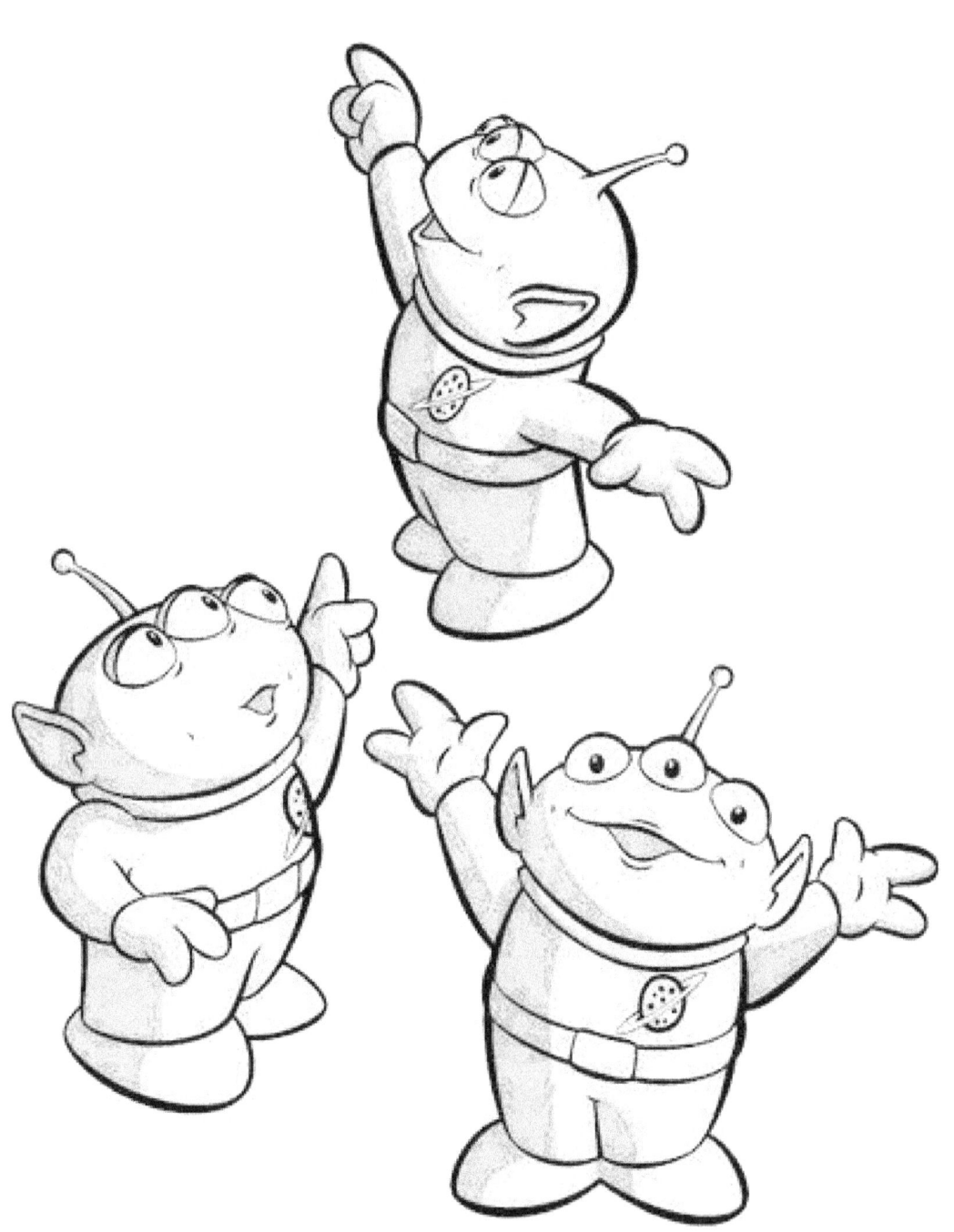

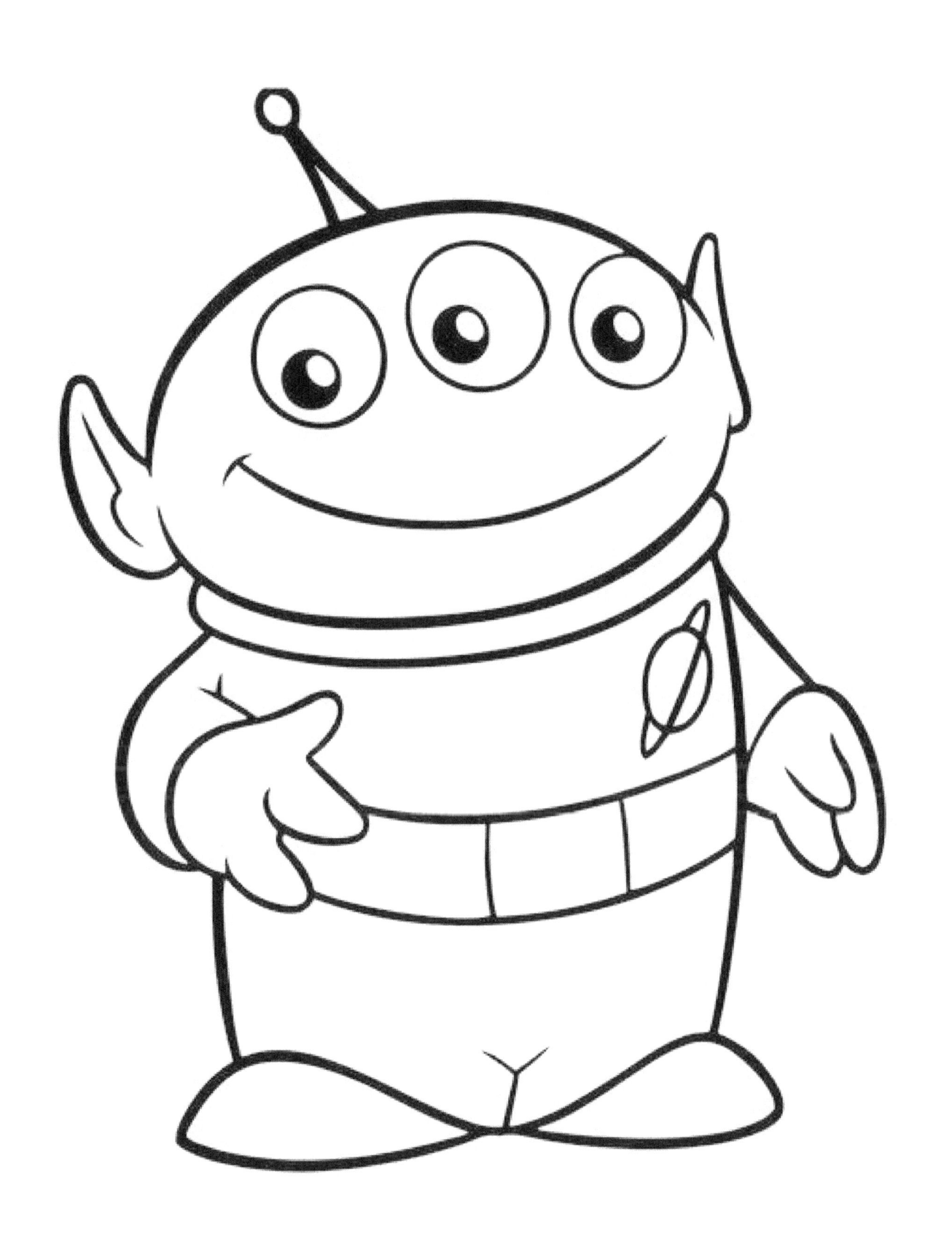

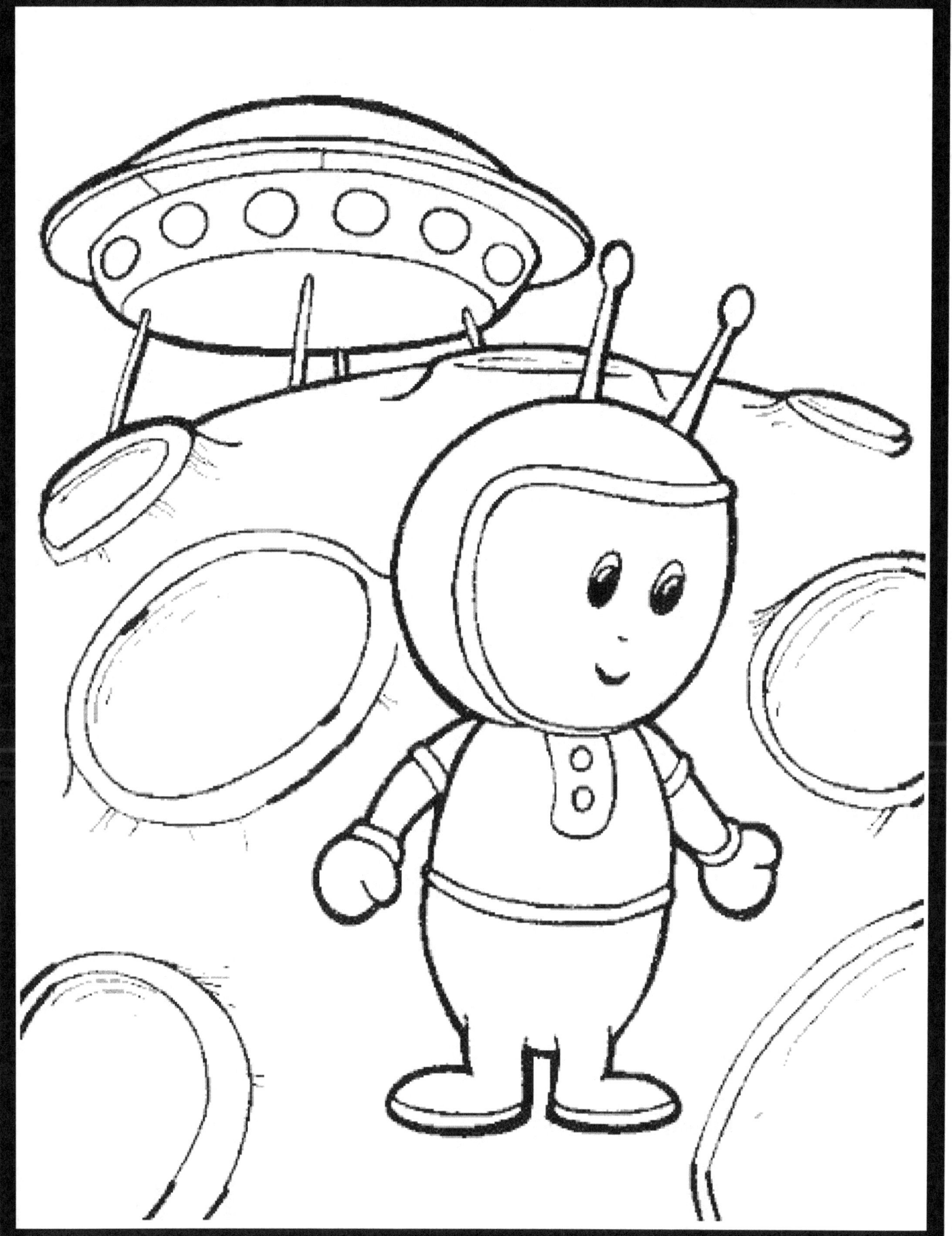

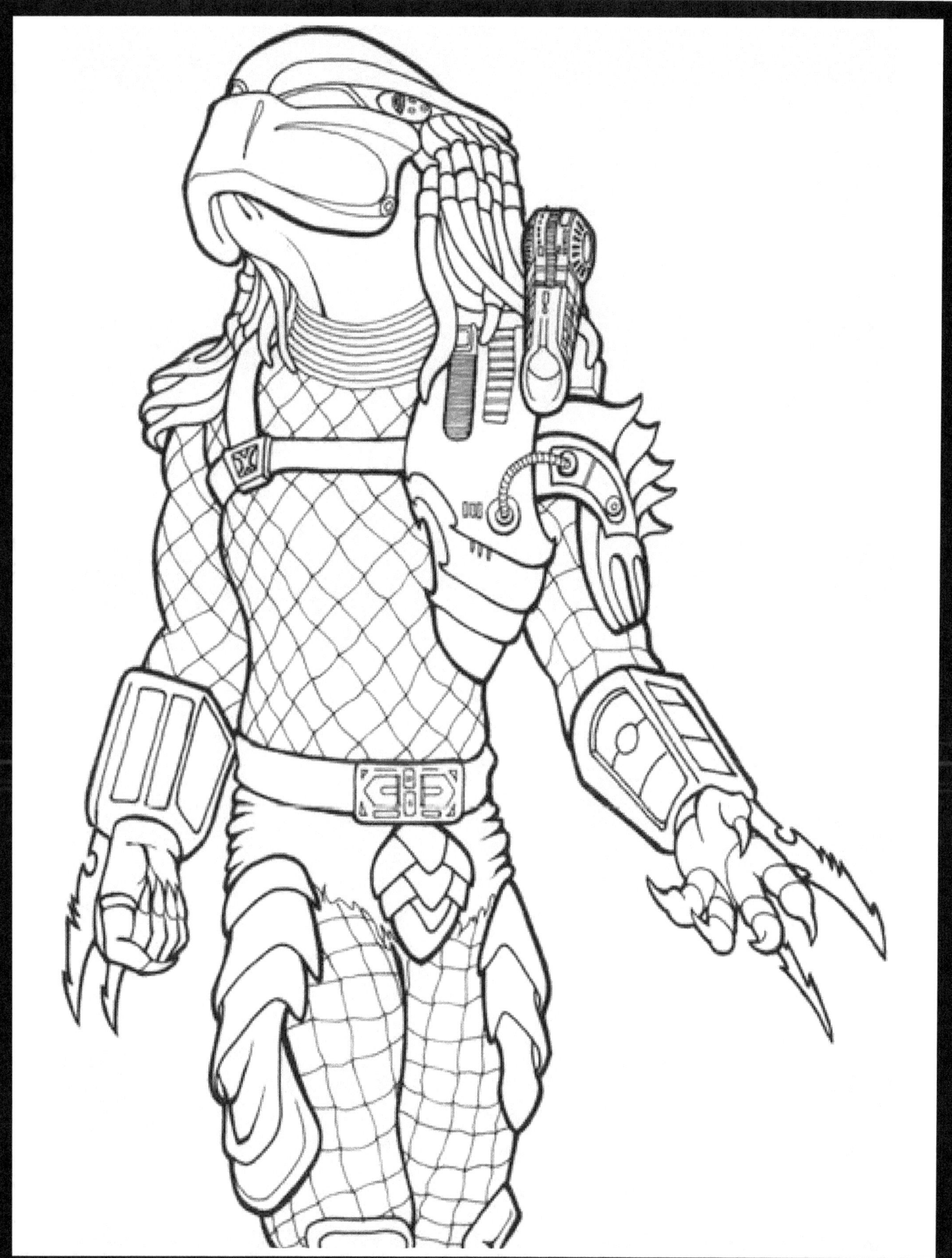

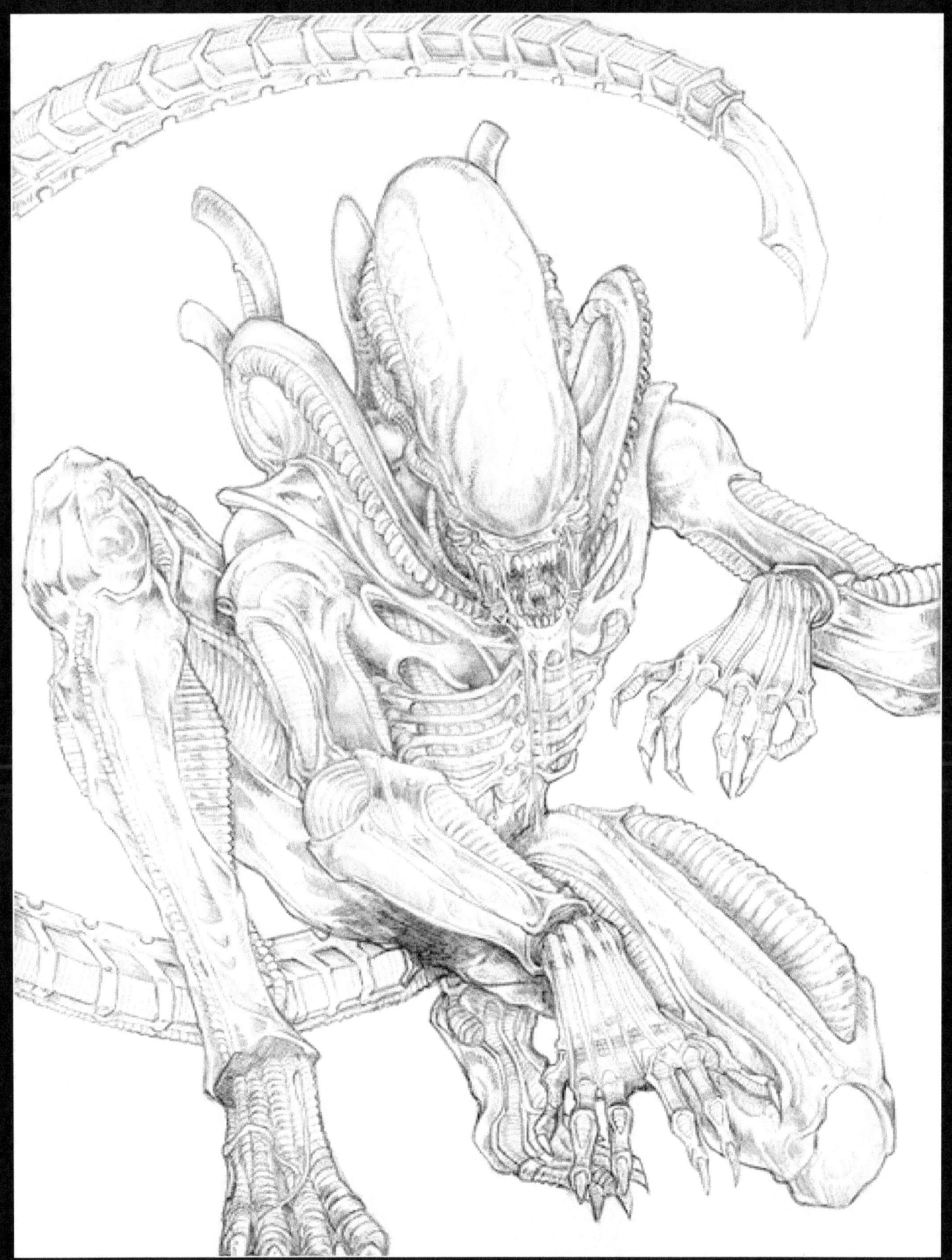

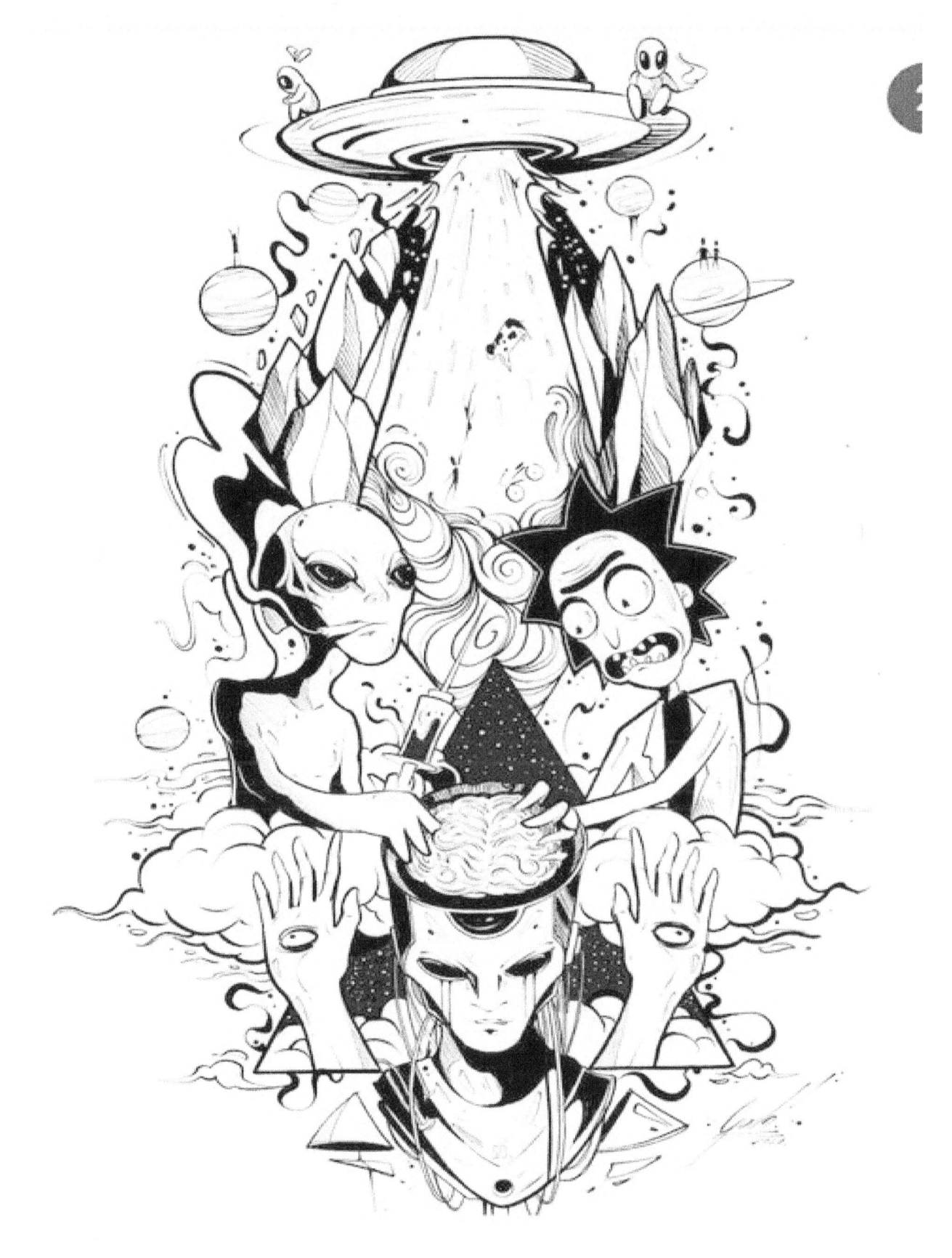

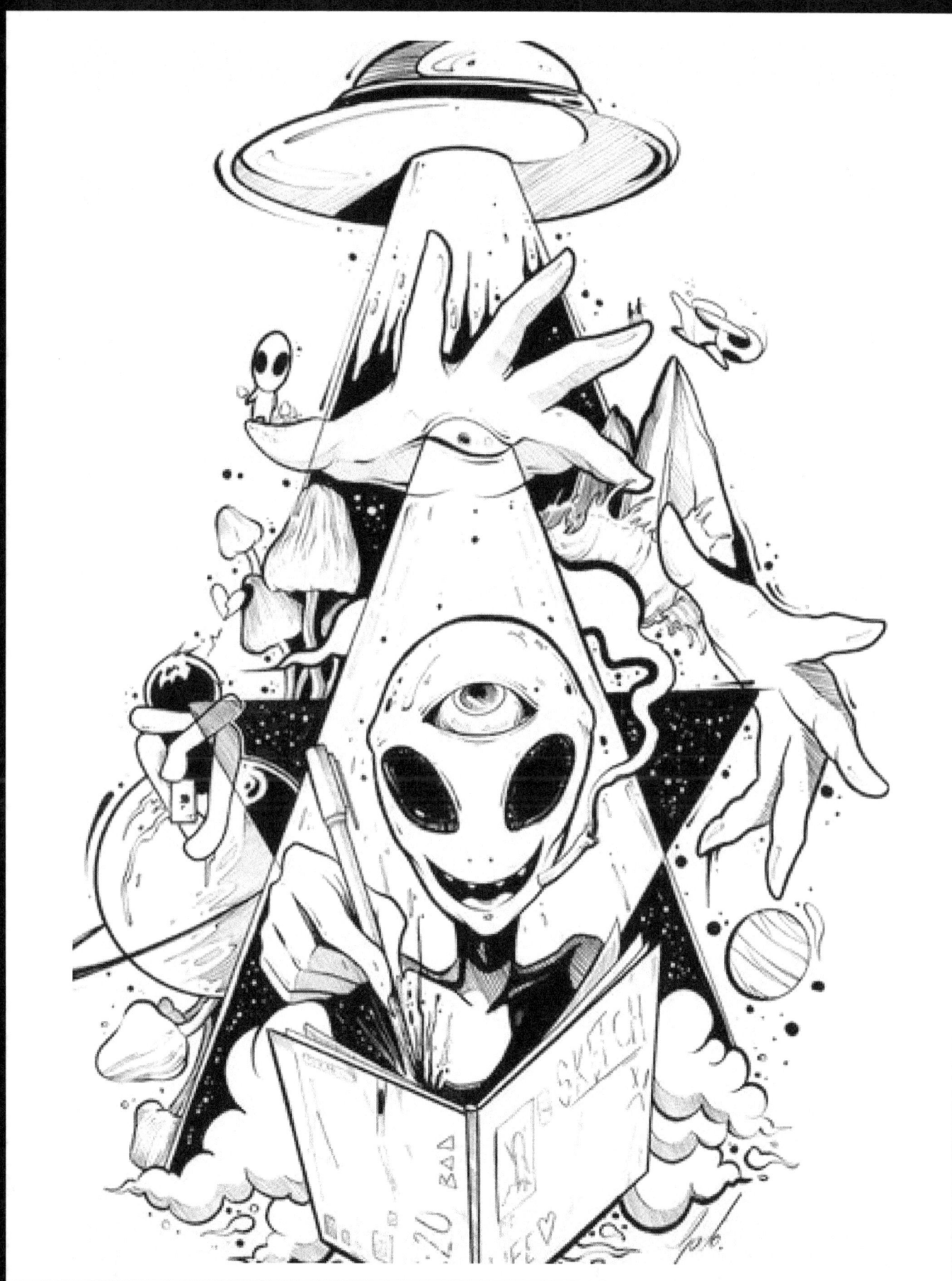

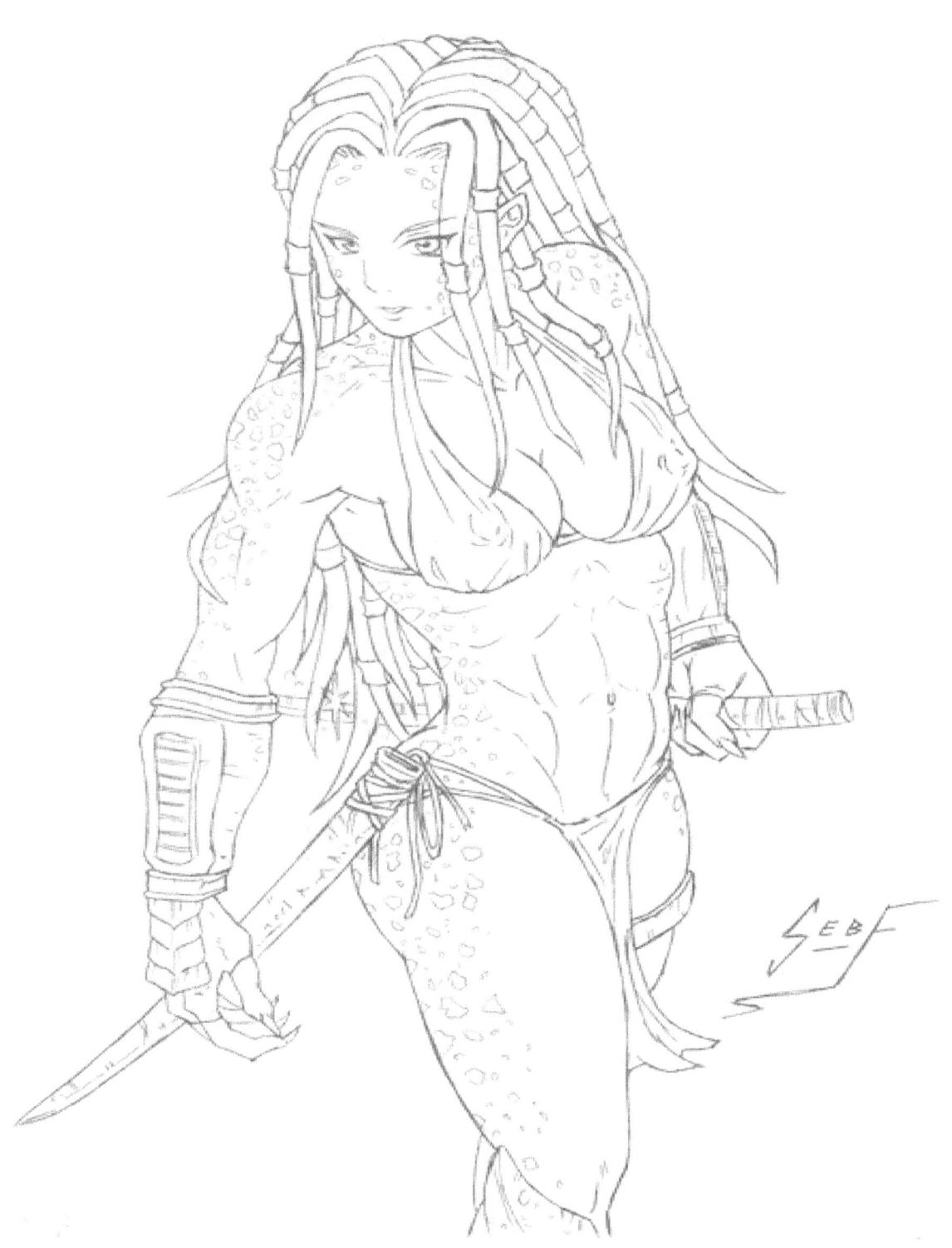

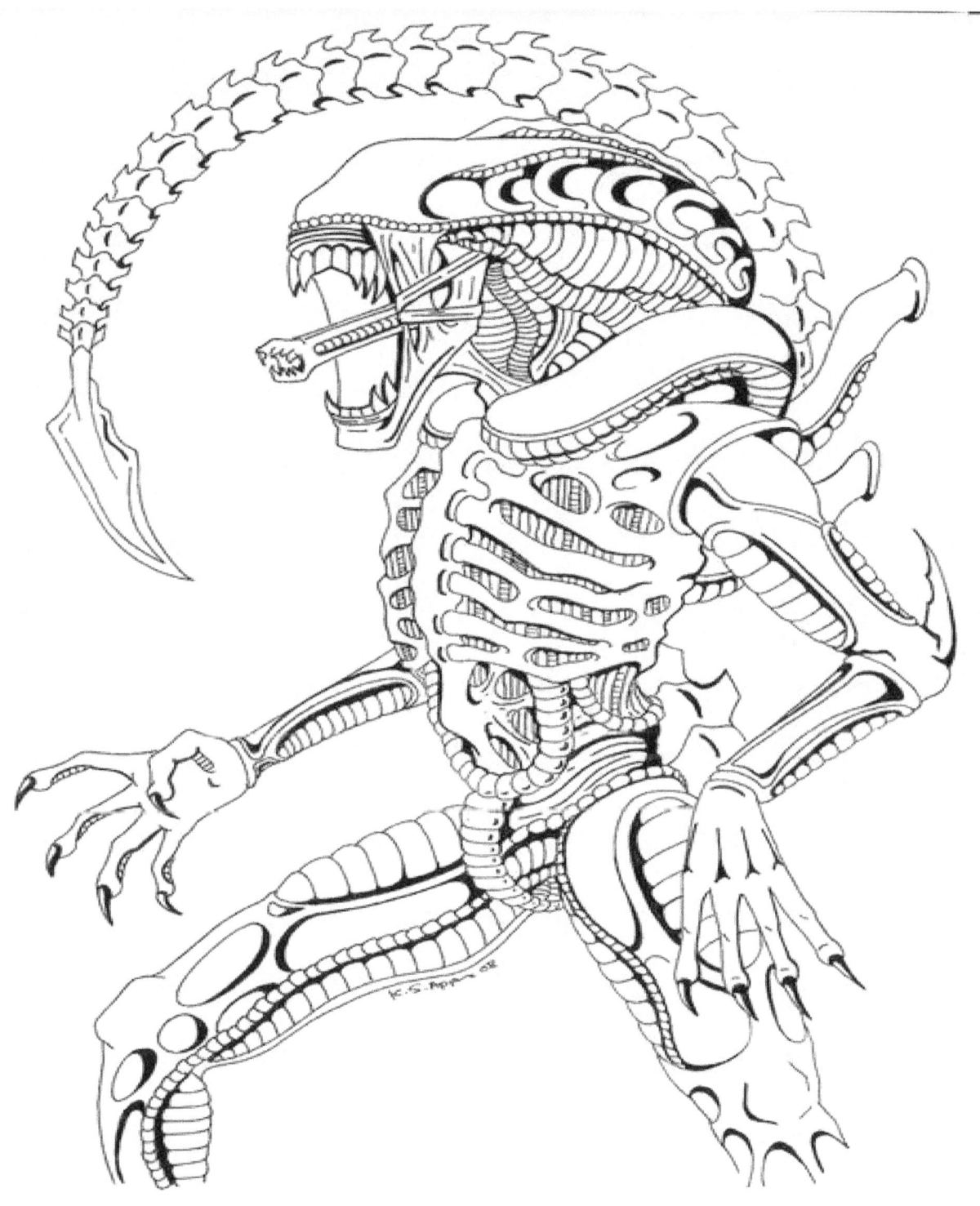

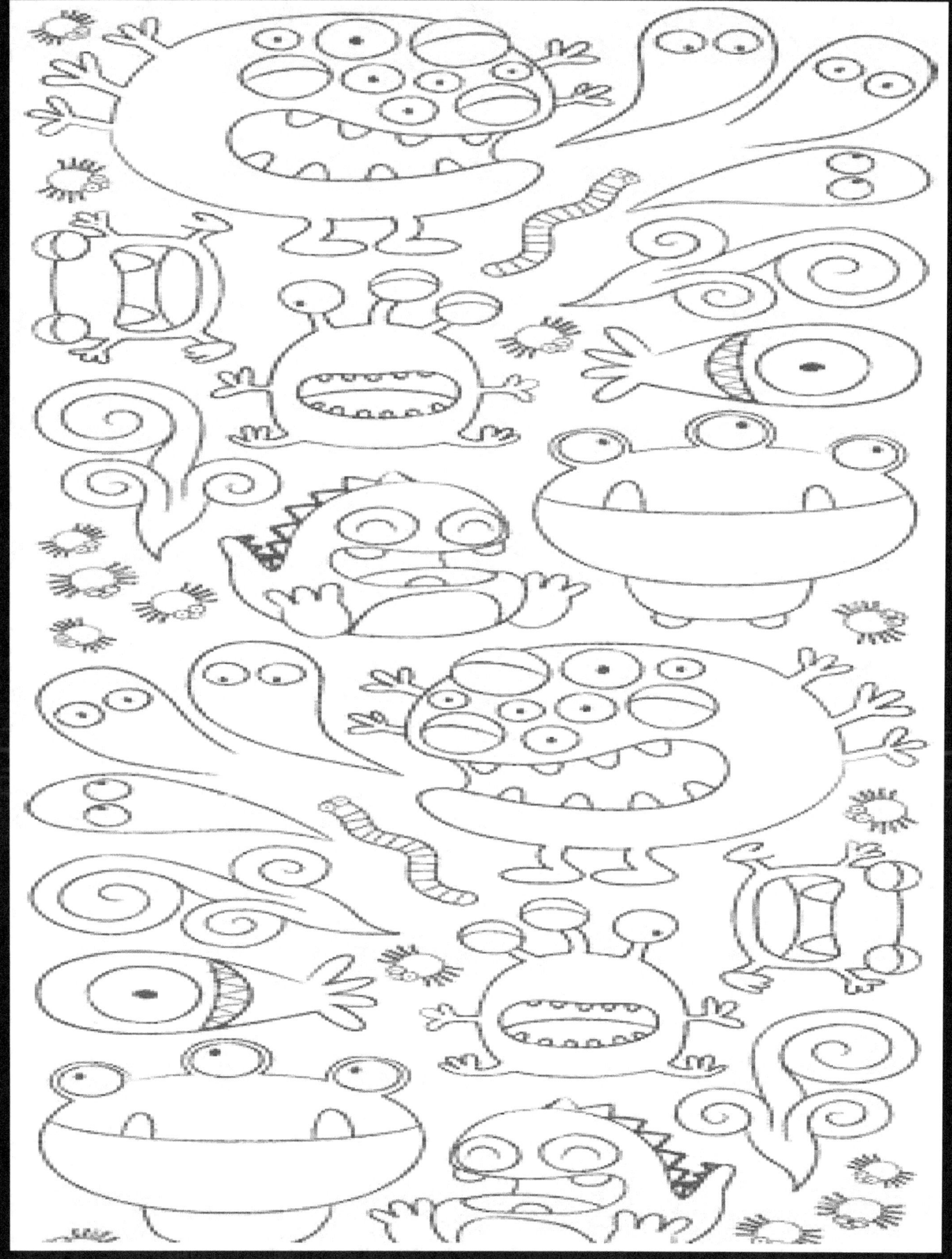

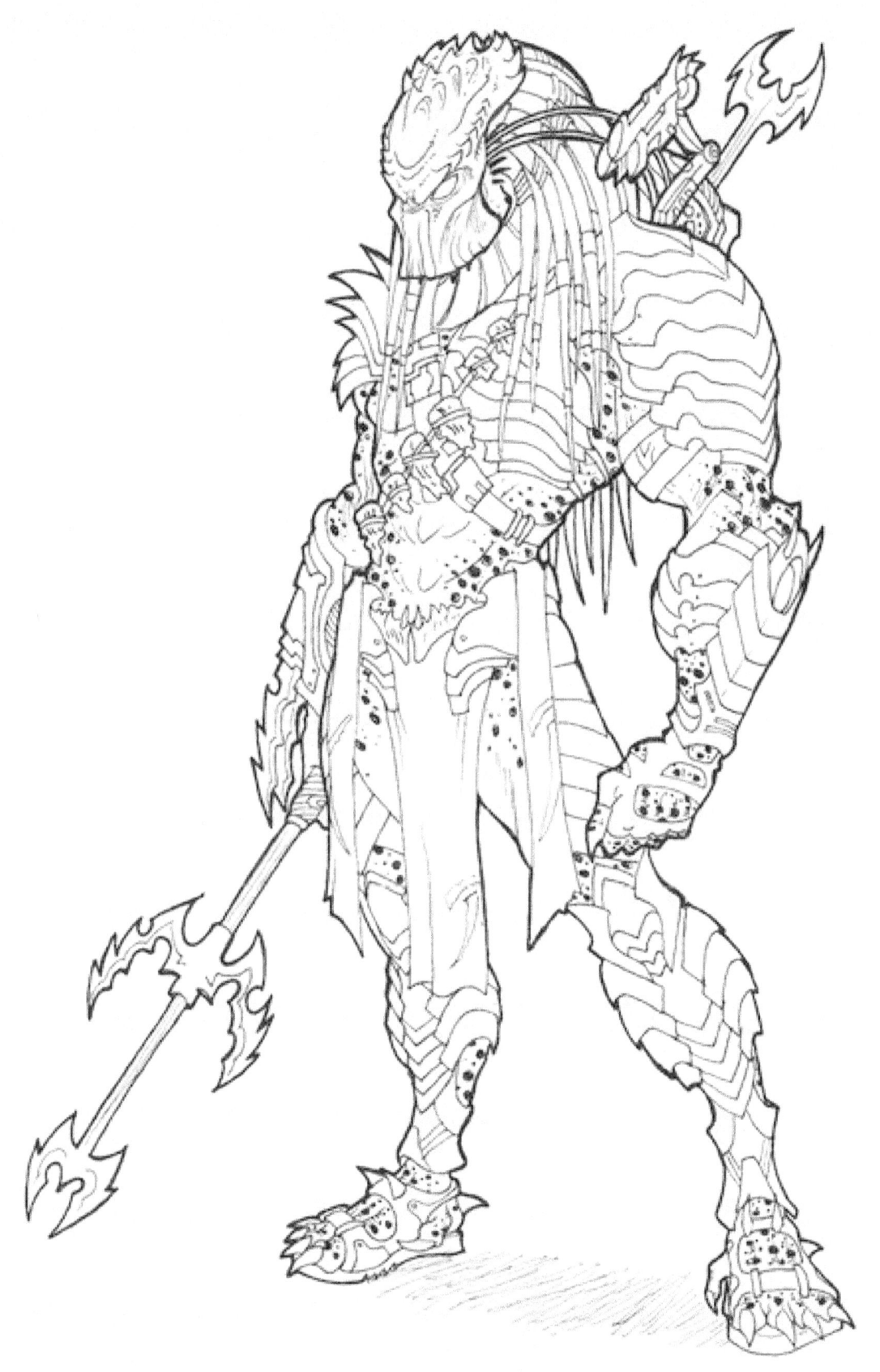

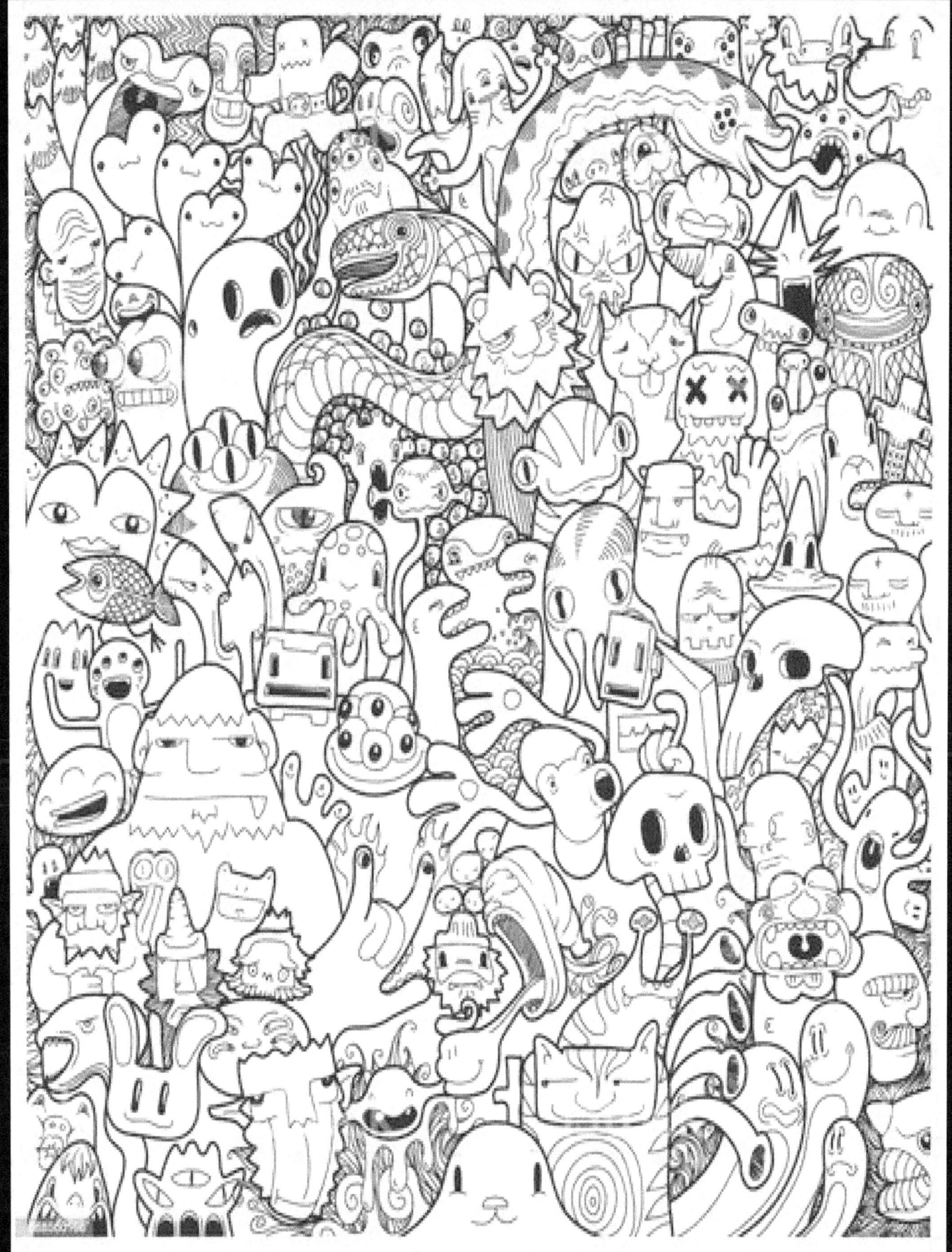

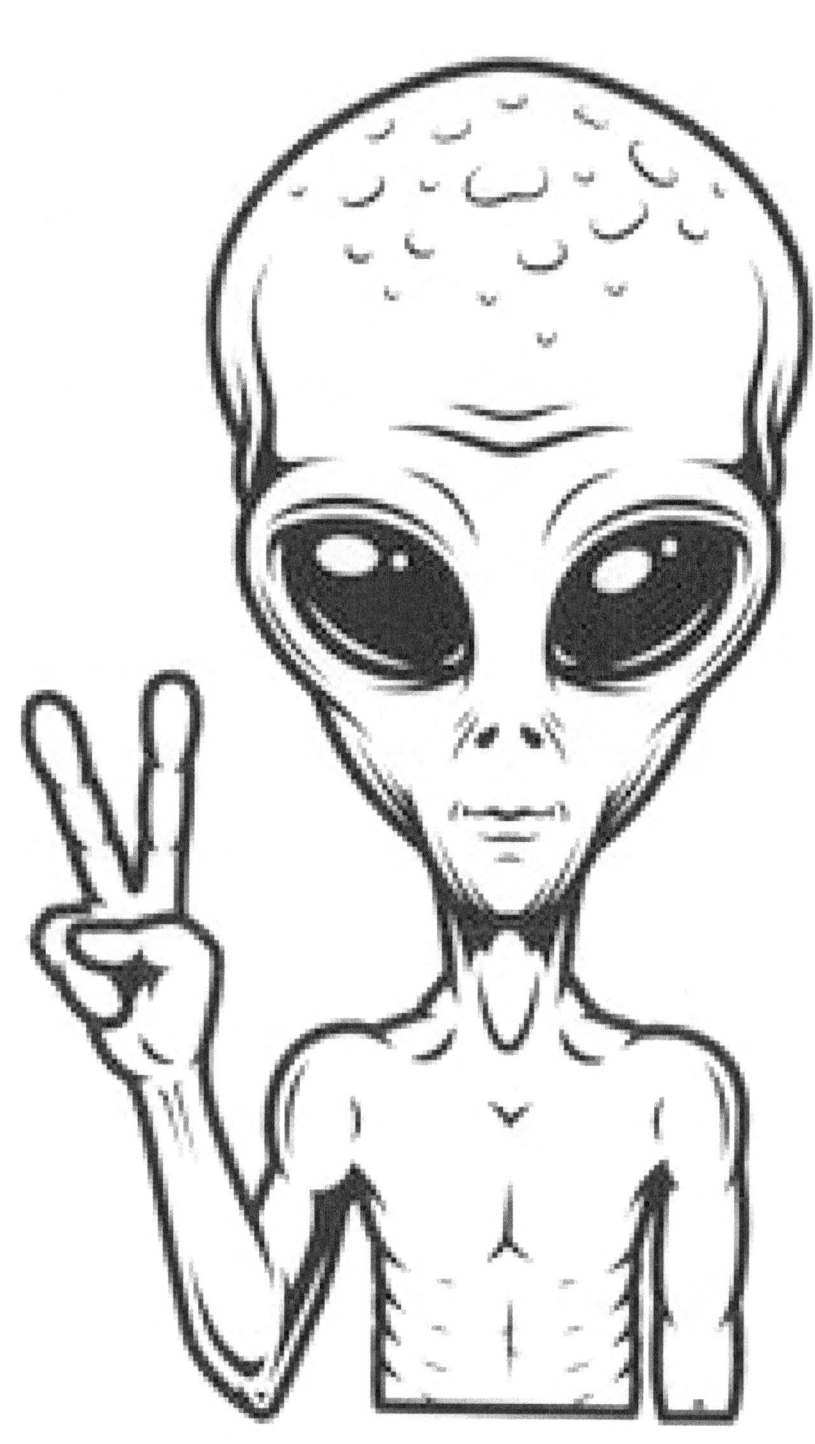

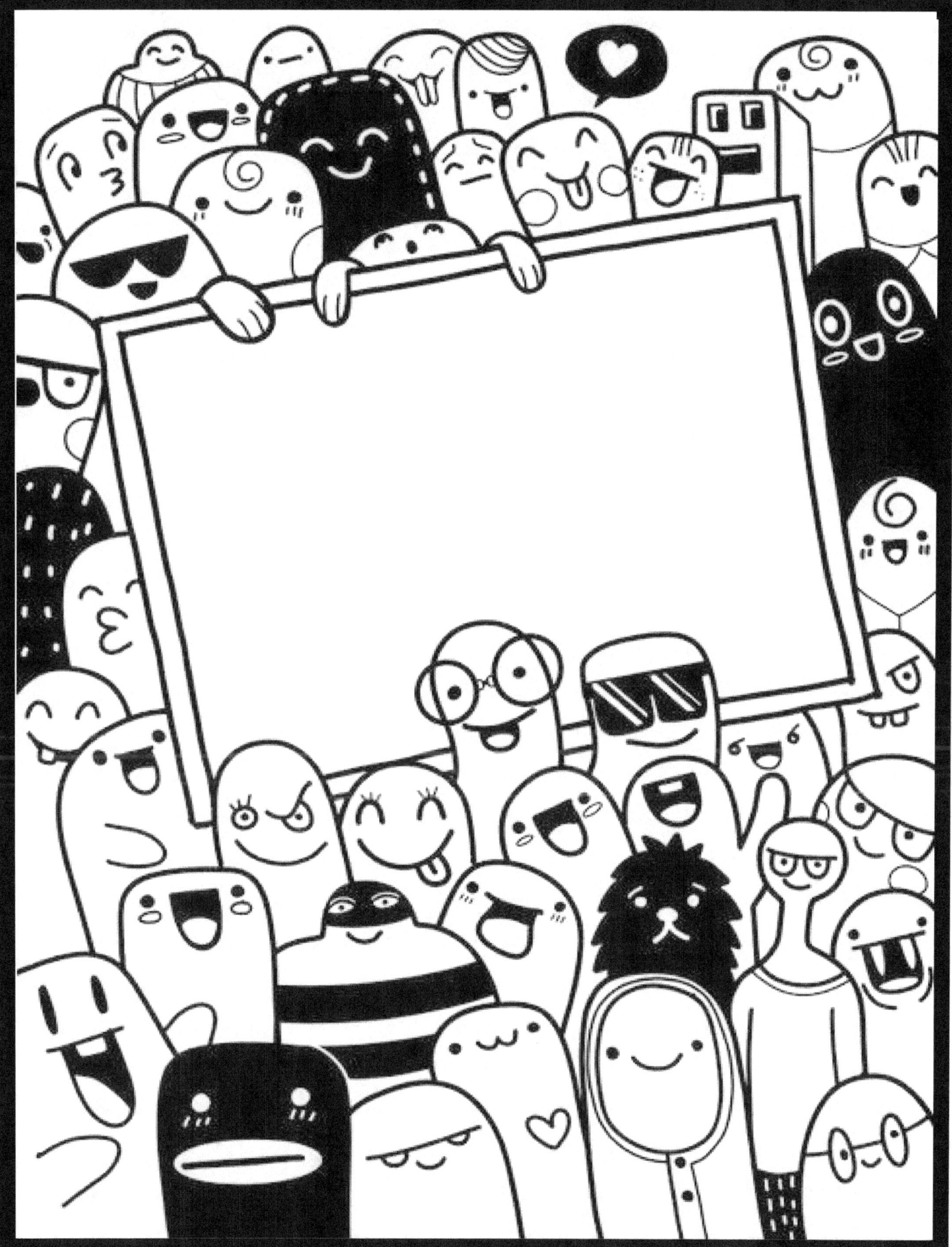

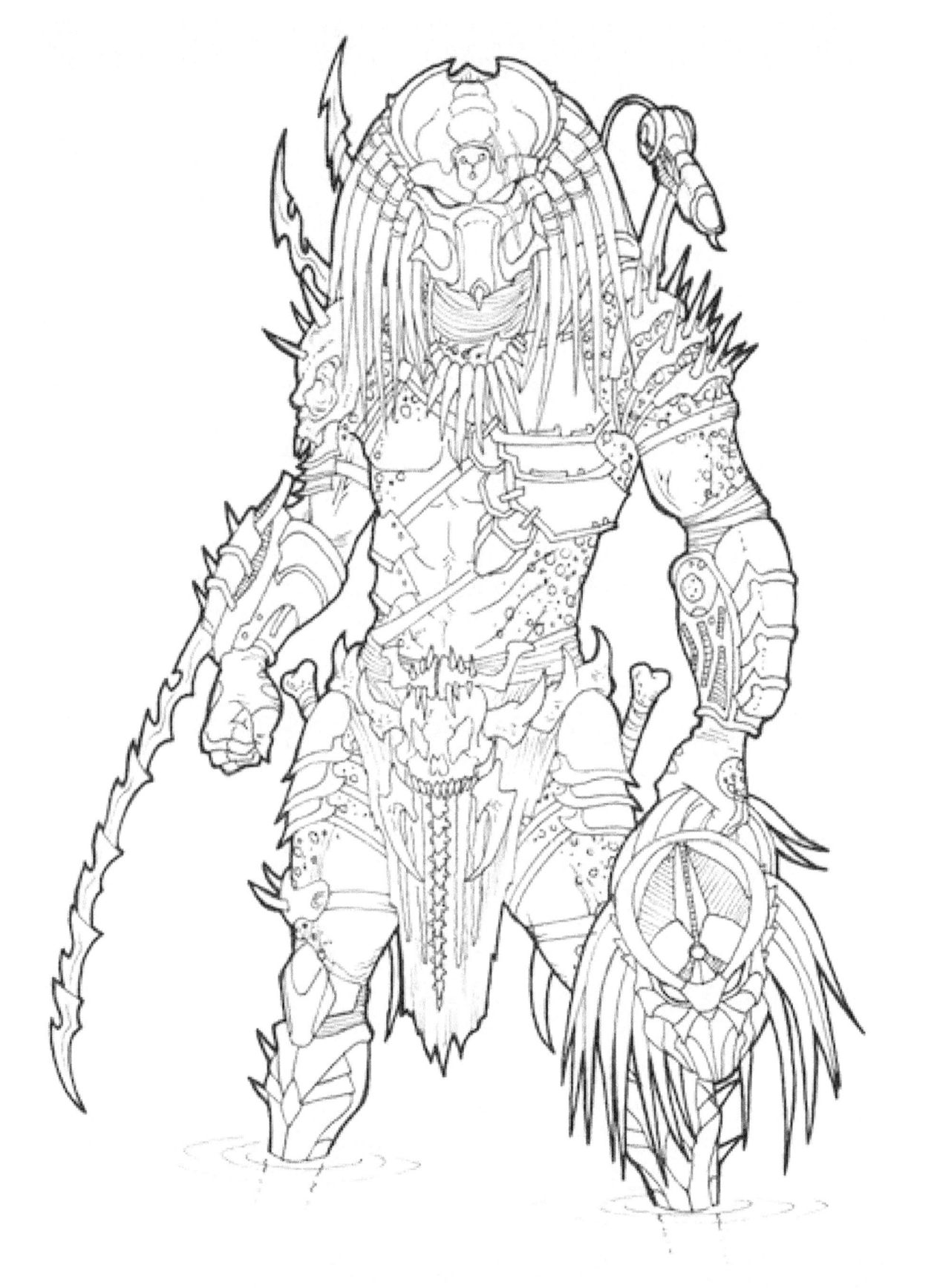

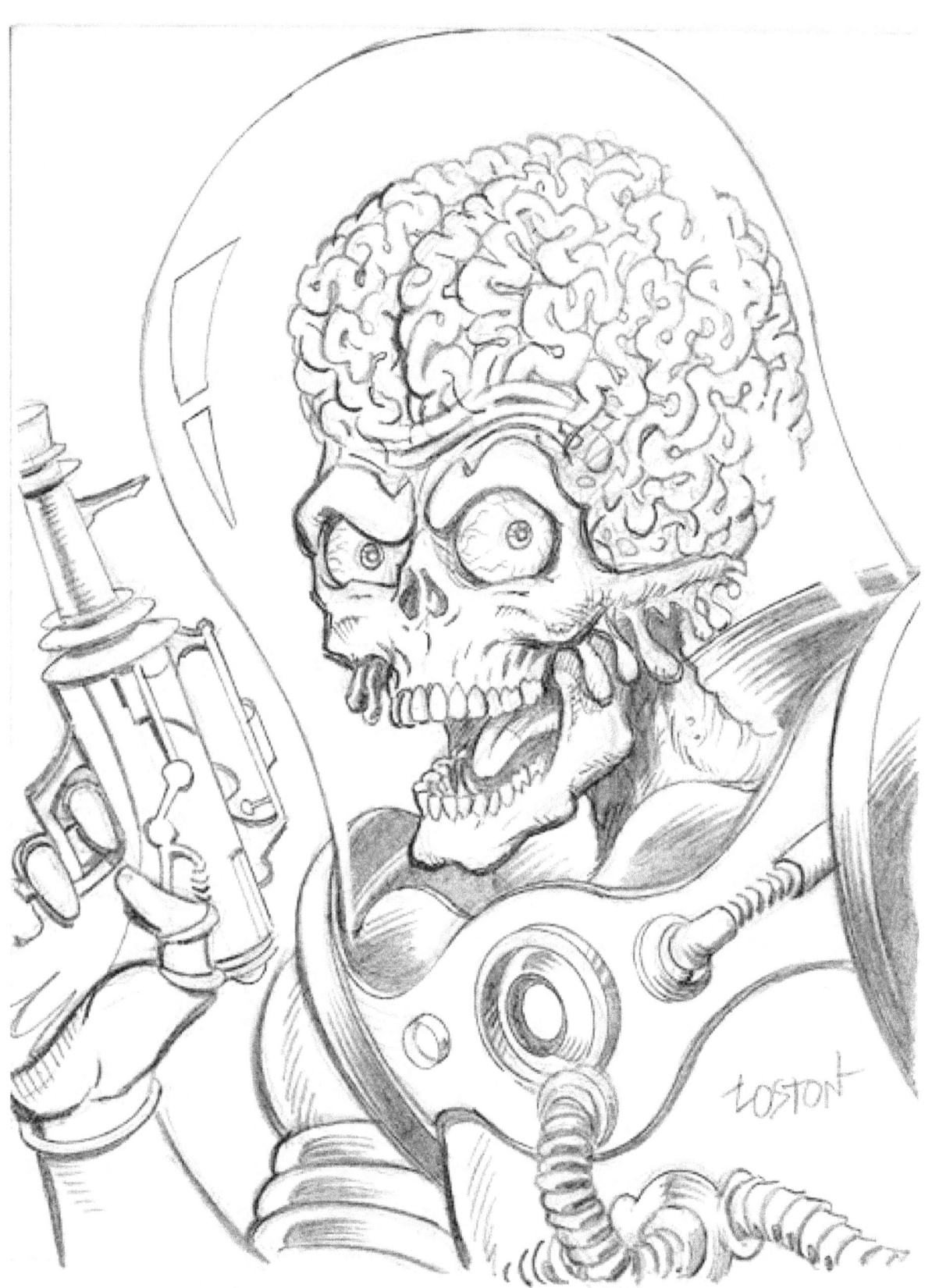

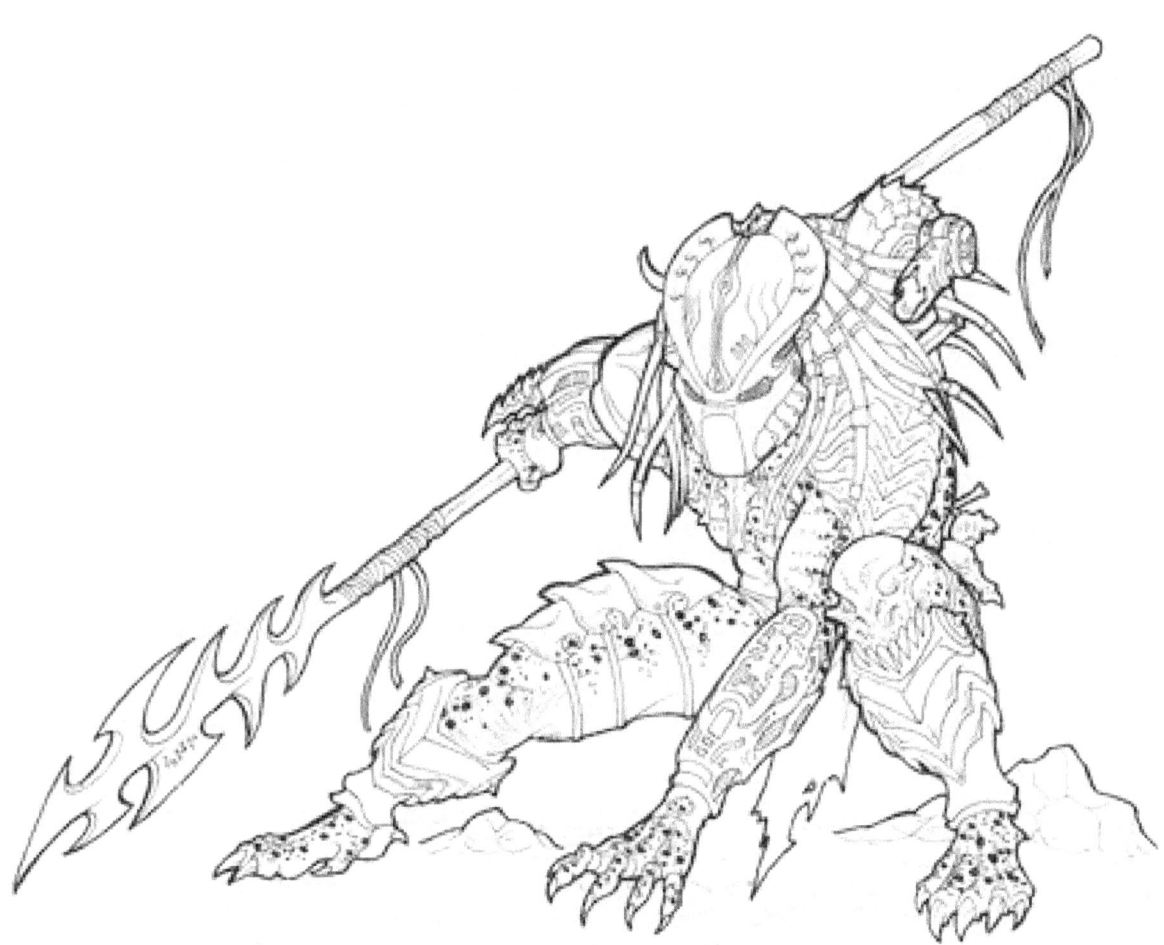

DRAW WHAT I LEARNED HERE

DRAW WHAT I LEARNED HERE

DRAW WHAT I LEARNED HERE

DRAW WHAT I LEARNED HERE

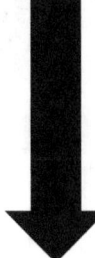

DRAW WHAT I LEARNED HERE

DRAW WHAT I LEARNED HERE

DRAW WHAT I LEARNED HERE

DRAW WHAT I LEARNED HERE

DRAW WHAT I LEARNED HERE

DRAW WHAT I LEARNED HERE

DRAW WHAT I LEARNED HERE

DRAW WHAT I LEARNED HERE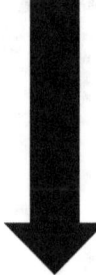

DRAW WHAT I LEARNED HERE

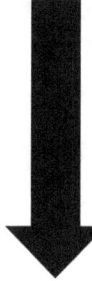

DRAW WHAT I LEARNED HERE

DRAW WHAT I LEARNED HERE

DRAW WHAT I LEARNED HERE

DRAW WHAT I LEARNED HERE

DRAW WHAT I LEARNED HERE

DRAW WHAT I LEARNED HERE

DRAW WHAT I LEARNED HERE

DRAW WHAT I LEARNED HERE

DRAW WHAT I LEARNED HERE

DRAW WHAT I LEARNED HERE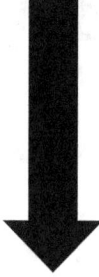

DRAW WHAT I LEARNED HERE